JACQUELINE KUCERA

Hey Man, Wake Up! Have You Been Framed?

5 Steps to Reclaim Your Freedom, Peace, Health and Respect

jacqueline@kucera.ch

First edition

ISBN: 9783952610220

This book was professionally typeset on Reedsy.
Find out more at reedsy.com

Thanks to my loving husband and my children for their constant support and love in everything I do.

I am grateful to my parents for pushing me out of my comfort zone to challenge and ultimately transcend deeply rooted beliefs, leading me on a path of self-discovery and purpose as I pursued higher goals, living my life with respect towards others and owning my own values.

I am not what happened to me, I am what I choose to become.
– Carl Jung –

Do not conform to the pattern of this world, but be transformed by the renewing of your mind.
– Romans 12:2 NIV –

Contents

Foreword

In *Hey Man, Wake Up! Have You Been Framed?* my mother, Jacqueline, offers a self-assured and hopeful invitation to any man feeling trapped by society's expectations.

Through five straightforward yet transformative steps, she reveals a practical blueprint for reclaiming freedom, peace, health and self-respect and living the life you truly want. Her guide challenges us to rethink what it means to live authentically.

Philippe Kucera

* * *

It's a privilege to revisit Jacqueline Kucera's work and share my excitement for her latest book, *Hey Man, Wake Up! Have You Been Framed?*

Timely, insightful, fierce and grounded, this book is more than an evaluation of the issues we're facing and how we got here; it's a humane and achievable solution.

As always, Jacqueline approaches her topic with nuance and compassion, recognising that men – in particular young men – also suffer under the weight of the outdated, oversimplified ideas of masculinity imposed upon them by society. She helpfully envisions these expectations as a frame with fixed sides, as the restrictive bars of a cage.

This book explores the origins of this rigid societal framing and the way it now works to hold people back from reaching their full potential. But there's a double meaning here too, where to be framed is to be pre-judged. An entrenching rhetoric that looks only for black and white makes assumptions of men and boys, which tighten the bars of the cage still further and keep them on this limiting, damaging path through life.

When we break the frame, we throw out these pre-judgements. This fresh start creates space for the uniqueness of every person and the complex dialogue necessary to navigate the issues of our volatile, uncertain, complex and ambiguous world.

What sets this book apart is Jacqueline's frank yet hopeful approach. She doesn't shy away from the structural challenges we face, and she presents her message in a way that's both constructive and practical. She's a problem-solver at her heart, and she offers her solution in five memorable, actionable lessons: *Reconnection*, *Freedom*, *Peace*, *Health* and *Respect.*

At every stage, she reflects on these lessons from the point of view of a man who has been denied these essential pillars for a fulfilled life, and with an eye on the potential for societal change if we reject the frames forced upon us and live with the inner respect, trust and love we should afford ourselves as human beings.

As with her first book, Jacqueline's voice shines with wisdom, drawn from her rich life experiences and relationships. Her work reflects a profound understanding of the challenges facing society and the changes that need to happen for us to address them together.

This book is essential reading for anyone seeking a candid but constructive evaluation of where we are and where we need to go. Whether you're a framed man, a teacher, a parent of boys or simply a person who senses that something is wrong with the way the world works, this book provides both clarity and direction.

It's time to wake up, break the frame and start building a better future – together.

Mairi Bunce

Preface

Hey man, wake up! Have you been framed?

This book is a transformative journey empowering every man to become his true inner self. It's an invitation to reconnect with yourself and leave behind the limitations imposed by external societal expectations.

Wake up and take the first step, break free from imposed frames and reclaim a life where freedom, peace, health and respect are yours to own.

Reading this book and reflecting on your journey could change your life.

Five Steps to Reclaim Your Freedom, Peace, Health and Respect

You are enough. As Carl Jung said, 'I am not what happened to me, I am what I choose to become.'

This book is a heartfelt guide for young men feeling trapped by patriarchal norms and societal constraints that they believe they have to conform to. Inspired by my brother, who endured the weight of a controlling father and an unhealthy social environment, I've woven together personal stories, research and insights from global thought leaders. Society's expectations can weigh heavily on boys and men, forcing them into roles that feel increasingly restrictive in a quickly evolving world.

In today's world, where social media and rapid change are shifting the way we see ourselves, outdated patriarchal roles and traditional social norms are crumbling. Men and women alike feel trapped, yearning to break free.

The term ' patriarchy' traditionally refers to a social system where men hold primary power, often resulting in the oppression of women. However, it's important to recognise that patriarchal structures can also be suppressive to men in various ways. Patriarchal norms impose strict definitions of masculinity, such as the idea that men must be emotionally stoic, aggressive and act as providers. The book *Guyland* by Michael Kimmel discusses the societal pressures on men to conform to a narrow definition of masculinity, which can lead to emotional distress and limit their personal choices.

In the concept of patriarchy, men are often discouraged from expressing vulnerability or deep emotional needs, which can lead to mental health issues and isolation. In *The Mask of Masculinity*, Lewis Howes examines how societal expectations trap men in a facade of toughness, leading to emotional challenges and loneliness.

Traditional gender roles can create unhealthy relationship dynamics, putting pressure on men to dominate. In the book *Men Are from Mars, Women Are from Venus*, John Gray explores how these dynamics can lead to misunderstandings and conflict, ultimately suggesting that both men and women suffer when rigid roles are imposed.

The expectation for men to prioritise work over parenting can also lead to regret and strain in family relationships. *The Way of the Peaceful Warrior* by Dan Millman speaks about the balance between work, personal life and the fulfillment that comes from nurturing relationships.

Patriarchal ideals can prevent men from being open to their vulnerabilities, leading to inauthentic lives. *Daring Greatly* by Brené Brown encourages us to embrace vulnerability and authenticity, highlighting the fact that true strength lies in being willing to show your true self.

Certain patriarchal laws and systems can also disadvantage men, such as biases in family court or employment discrimination. *The Second Sex* by Simone de Beauvoir explores how societal structures disadvantage both women and men in various ways and advocates for a more equitable understanding.

In this book, drawing on the works of several authors, I share my own journey to recognising how men, too, are often suppressed by societal expectations in family life, society and the workplace.

Growing up, my brother and I were inseparable. He, with his curly brown hair, was the family's golden child when he was young, while I stood out in my own way. We were best friends, believing in limitless possibilities, only to be constrained by rigid social norms and self-doubt as we grew older. His story reflects the struggle for freedom, the search for purpose and the toll it takes. At fifteen, my brother's path led him to a career as a DJ, but behind his achievements was a yearning for more, a search for himself. Sadly, he left us at just thirty-six, a loss that shattered our family and left a lasting impact on everyone who knew him.

This book aims to inspire you to think about your own path: what does it mean to live freely, peacefully and with respect for yourself? How can we find our true selves beneath society's pressures?

Drawing inspiration from Steven Kotler, Sky Nelson-Isaacs, James Clear, Daniel Paul Woodring and other authors, this book offers five transformative steps to reconnect with your inner self and escape the limitations imposed by society. You'll learn how to harness your choices to shape a life of flow, how to build self-respect and how to create habits that align with peace and purpose.

Take this journey. Follow the five steps to *Reconnection*, *Freedom*, *Peace*,

Health and *Respect* and start living a life defined by harmony and meaning. This book calls on young men to realise that they might be framed by expectations from those around them, living in an environment they didn't choose.

Wake up, break free from imposed frames and reclaim a life where freedom, peace, health and respect are yours to own.

Prologue

Disruption and Transformation

A Story from the 1960s to 2025

Looking back on my life, from a childhood in Switzerland to the present day, I am struck by how fast the world has changed – often in ways that seemed unimaginable.

Growing up in the 1970s, life was simpler in many ways: no mobile phones, no internet and a black-and-white television serving as our sole window to the wider world. Rapid and constant changes have taken place between the 1960s and today, and the relentless pace of transformation within all the fields of our lives has swept us into a future that is at once thrilling and overwhelming. This is the story of decades of disruption and transformation.

In the 1960s, the patriarchy in Europe began to be challenged as both women and men started questioning traditional gender roles. Women sought greater autonomy and equality, influenced by the post-war shift where they entered the workforce in large numbers and resisted returning to traditional roles. The sexual revolution, with the advent of the pill, gave women control over their bodies, while feminist thinkers – like Simone de Beauvoir in the *Second Sex* or Judith Butler in *Gender Trouble* – challenged patriarchal norms with the discussion of the performativity of gender.

At the same time, young men were also grappling with societal expectations that limited emotional expression and personal identity. Influenced by the global civil rights and student movements, young men began to question the rigid norms of masculinity that restricted so much of their inner lives.

This movement was addressed all over the world, including in Switzerland. David Eugster describes the situation in Switzerland at the time: 'The rules governing how men and women behaved with one another became freer, and education gradually moved away from corporal punishment and authoritarian discipline.'

Following that social and student movement, Switzerland witnessed a turning point, with the women's movement fighting for equality and the right to vote – a milestone that was finally achieved in 1971. The movement gained momentum alongside growing discontent among young men who were seeking more freedom from traditional masculine roles. This shift, fuelled by increased educational opportunities and global feminist activism, created a more open space for both women and young men to challenge societal norms and fight for more inclusive, balanced identities.

It was an era of social awakening, and as traditional gender roles began to be questioned, society embraced a cautious optimism for change. The seeds of progress were planted, even as the world continued to feel stable and predictable compared to today. We believed that the patriarchy was dead.

The 1980s arrived with both turbulence and innovation. Economic crises rippled across the globe, shaking the stable foundations. At the same time, early personal computers began to emerge. These machines hinted at the dawn of a digital era, promising to redefine the way we worked and interacted in ways we were only beginning to imagine.

The 1990s brought their own challenges, particularly economic struggles, but technology continued its steady march forward. Portable phones began to appear, marking the early stages of a connected future that would soon reshape human interaction. This period felt like a transition, a bridge to something transformative.

With the 2000s came the explosion of social media and the ubiquity of mobile phones. Suddenly, the way we connected with one another changed completely, and the world underwent a dramatic shift. Relationships and careers moved online, creating both opportunities and unforeseen challenges. At the same time, the global banking crisis revealed the vulnerability of even the most powerful economic systems, exposing cracks in what many assumed to be unshakable institutions.

By the 2010s, climate change had taken centre stage as one of humanity's greatest challenges. Activism and public awareness forced us to confront our environmental impact, though meaningful progress was slow. Meanwhile, technology advanced at a dizzying pace. Smartphones, artificial intelligence (AI) and big data were becoming more relevant. With big data – an increased efficiency in data and information handling – and more access to digitally provided information, everyone in the world was able to connect at all times to any information. Communication became straight forward – shorter, quicker, more agile and independent of time and place. This evolution led to changes in society, creating the need for communication through social networks. The meaning of work and free time began to shift.

Now, in the 2020s, we find ourselves facing a world shaped by AI and automation. These technologies bring extraordinary potential but also spark new ethical, social and democratic dilemmas. Machines are increasingly intertwined with our lives as they are advising us, shaping our thoughts and beliefs and organising our routines. Autonomous systems can make independent decisions, acting as 'agents' in a world where human oversight is no longer guaranteed. As robots and AI take on more human-like roles, we face difficult questions about control, purpose and identity in a hyper-automated future where steering our own lives becomes even more challenging.

For young men, today's world is dominated by social media, gaming consoles and virtual interactions. Platforms like Instagram, TikTok and X offer endless connections and global communities, yet they often leave a sense of disconnection, a widening gap between online life and tangible reality. The challenge lies in bridging this divide, rediscovering authentic relationships and grounding ourselves in the physical world.

Reflecting on these decades, one thing becomes clear: we must take ownership of our lives. From a world without mobile phones to today's volatile digital landscape, we now live in a VUCA world – volatile, uncertain, complex and ambiguous. The future can feel unpredictable, even daunting, but it's ours to shape.

The lessons of the past, perseverance, adaptability and the power of collective effort remain invaluable tools. So, take your life into your own hands today. Embrace the opportunities of this ever-changing world, meet its challenges head-on and chart a path towards a future that reflects your values and aspirations. The story of disruption and transformation is not over, as you'll find through your own development into a more authentic person. It's up to you to determine the course.

Old norms are being questioned and replaced by others, and yet the dominating concept of patriarchy is still prevalent. Let's break free from it. Let's not be held by the patriarchal constraints and stifling societal norms, and let's embrace a life of true self-reconnection.

This book is your guide to reclaiming your Freedom, Peace, Health and Respect in just five steps. Because, in the end, you are not defined by what has happened to you; you are who you choose to become.

Wake up, man! Take your life into your own mind!

Introduction

From the moment we enter the world, our minds begin forming intricate neural pathways that guide our actions and encode our values, shaped profoundly by the people and systems around us. As Steven Kotler illustrates in *The Art of Impossible*, these pathways develop in our early years through curiosity and openness. But as we grow older, social pressures and, in many contexts, patriarchal norms gradually impose beliefs and behaviours that we can internalise without realising their full impact on our self-identity (see Woodring). In adult life, we would be able to continue to learn from our mistakes. However, in our rigid society, mistakes are no longer allowed. This has an impact on our behaviour, as we try to avoid errors and thus comply with the intended behaviour.

In today's digital landscape, this conditioning is intensified. We increasingly turn to social media and AI tools like ChatGPT for information and affirmation, often placing more trust in screens than in one another. Such reliance raises urgent questions about how these technologies affect our relationships: by seeking reassurance from machines, do we risk weakening genuine human bonds, trading real connection for a curated, surface-level reality?

Kenneth Gergen, in *The Saturated Self*, highlights how these online interactions, often fragmented and idealised, shape our sense of who we are. Meanwhile, Kotler's concept of 'ferocity' captures the clash between empowering genuine personal growth and chasing superficial praise. We can aspire to discipline and grit, yet we find ourselves regularly involved in social media consumption, hoping for digital approval. Running after these distant digital rewards, we have no time to engage in more meaningful relationships in our lives.

Consider how freely we move through life as children. We explore the world without filters or self-imposed limits, guided by curiosity and an unguarded sense of possibility. But as we mature, these open horizons shrink under the weight of social norms and unspoken rules, many of them bolstered by the patriarchal assumptions that constrain our potential. Over time, we adapt, often unconsciously, to fit expectations that might not truly reflect who we are.

Where does this path lead? Frequently, it culminates in limiting beliefs that we inherit rather than choose. Picture a once-curious child gradually conforming to the rigidity around him/her until he/she scarcely recognises their original sense of self. In patriarchal and oppressive systems, these restrictions tighten further, binding us to inherited roles and narrow definitions of worth and being. Why, then, do we yield to these patterns, and why do we let social structures decide our value and the way we have to lead our lives?

In our hyper-connected yet emotionally distant world, the virtual 'likes' and 'follows' of social media increasingly substitute for authentic human contact. Many of our interactions never progress beyond a digital interface, dulling our ability to engage meaningfully. As Johan Hari recounts, people can share life-altering news and receive only cursory responses because everyone is too absorbed in their own feed to recognise genuine human need.

And so we arrive at a paradox. On one hand, evolving technologies offer unprecedented opportunities and the chance to connect even when parted. On the other, they risk reinforcing the very societal norms – particularly patriarchal and constraining ones, as well as stereotypes – that hinder us from living freely and authentically.

In our society, men often still live in a male-dominated world. Filling up social media and AI chatbots with their ideas and belief systems, they program those tools with patriarchal norms and reinforce the stereotypes of this world. Why would we allow our tools to define our lives and our purposes, aligning us with values that might clash with our deepest beliefs?

Social media embodies this dilemma. While it can foster connection, its promise of instant affirmation often comes at the expense of deeper bonds.

By depending on likes and comments and a false sense of connection, social media gives us a gateway to escape the true, sometimes harsh nature of life. It gives us the opportunity to turn our brains off. We overlook the fact that we have to expose ourselves to the vulnerability and emotional investment required to nurture true and real relationships.

Adapting to our digital age calls for more than passive acceptance. We need resilience, curiosity and the courage to question and unlearn the things that don't serve us.

Are you currently in a situation where you say that you want to change, but you don't really want to, or you don't really have the courage to do so? Why? It's because pursuing a life that is more in line with how you envision it is more difficult than a life of comfort.

Go within and find your inner fire. This will tell you what you really burn for, which will be the light that shows you what you get up for in the morning.

To start, you need the courage to step up and say loudly to yourself, 'Just do it!' Only then can you break free from society's limiting scripts and reclaim your inherent power to live in alignment with your true self.

Are you living for you or for someone else's expectations? Are your aspirations truly yours, or are they buried under layers of social conditioning?

How can you stay human in a world shaped by technology? Do we trust digital sources more than one another? What does this mean for the authenticity of our relationships and for who we're becoming?

Why is this Important?

Young men today seem to feel increasingly lost, drawn to social media, digital interactions and immersive (sometimes violent) gaming as a way to feel like they belong. They might begin to believe that these online connections define friendship and community. But how can communities formed only through profiles, likes and comments on platforms truly create a sense of belonging and build relationships?

Psychological studies and the work of authors like Karla Elliott and Jean Twenge reveal that many young men feel pressured to conform to society's expectations of masculinity – to be tough and independent. Terrence Real's research on male depression shows how these societal expectations often push boys and men to hide their feelings, disconnecting them from their emotions and from one another. Without healthy opportunities for expression, many experience an internal struggle to belong and end up feeling even more alienated. Social media can amplify this problem. As Twenge highlights in *iGen*, boys can rely on digital validation to feel included, but these online engagements often lack the emotional depth necessary for real friendships and can ultimately increase feelings of loneliness.

Scientific research highlights the way that patriarchal systems, with their rigid ideals of masculinity, deeply impact young men and boys. Real's work reveals that pressure to appear 'tough' and without emotion leads to hidden struggles with isolation and depression, as young men are discouraged from seeking support. Elliott and Niobe Way further emphasise that societal expectations push young men to suppress their vulnerability, limiting their ability to form genuine connections and leading to a profound 'crisis of connection'. Similarly, Joseph Pleck's concept of 'gender role strain' illustrates the internal conflict boys face when trying to meet traditional masculine standards. This type of behaviour can also result from fathers (or parents). When the child expresses their emotions, the father says, 'No, don't feel that way,' especially for so-called negative emotions. This could lead the child to inherently supress these emotions. Thus, the child is not given the ability to cope with such emotions, doesn't learn to cope with them, and will therefore not be able to cope with them. Later, they might resort to other means of 'self-medication', whether that is social media or other drugs.

When you constantly suppress parts of who you are or do what others expect, it's easy to lose touch with your authentic inner self. This might result not only from a child's social environment but also from the parents. Parents might disapprove of the dreams and aspirations of their children, so young men begin to adopt the behaviours and values of those around them just to feel like they 'fit in', even if these choices don't resonate with their own ideas and values. This silence isn't just lonely; it also shapes an identity based on external expectations rather than inner values. This leaves you with the feeling that you're playing a role rather than aspiring to your own dreams and living a life true to who you are.

But remember that who you are isn't defined by the rules society gives you; it's defined by the values, dreams and passions that genuinely matter to you. Your journey begins with allowing yourself to recognise your emotions and reflect on what they're telling you. Your feelings aren't weaknesses; they're clues, insights into what's important in your life and what might need to change. Embracing them and exploring what they reveal about you is the first step to creating a life that truly reflects your inner self.

In this journey towards self-discovery, it's essential to stay connected to what makes us human. As we enter a world increasingly shaped by technology and digital engagement, it's easy to lose sight of real relationships. Twenge warns that while these tools can offer instant validation, they can't replace the depth of face-to-face interactions and the respect and empathy that form the basis of genuine friendships. True friendships aren't made through scrolling and virtual achievements; they're built in real conversations, shared experiences and honest exchanges.

With the rise of powerful tools like AI, we need to ensure that these advancements serve us rather than shape us in ways that distance us from our own humanity. Technology can certainly assist us in many tasks, but it's important to remain aware that our humanity should stay at the core of how we interact with these tools.

By taking charge of designing a life that's true to you, you not only empower yourself but also challenge the outdated systems around you. So reflect on whether patriarchal norms still reinforce your behaviour, leading you to a place where you can't express your true self.

As you reflect on your journey, how does the challenge of transforming patriarchal systems into flat, consensus-oriented organisations resonate with you?

Do you believe that we're on the verge of a new social order and a new way of organising society and work? How important is this transformation, and what impact does it have on inclusiveness and equality in the workplace?

Five Steps to Get Back to Your Inner Self

Can you recall your childhood? The emotions that filled you, the dreams you cherished, and that powerful feeling that anything was possible? Back then, your imagination turned effortlessly into visions, those visions felt as real as if they were already achieved and you were the hero of your own story. What created that feeling? And how did you believe so deeply in your dreams?

As we grow older, we often lose touch with this powerful inner connection. Life circumstances, especially the weight of societal expectations, gradually impose themselves on us, pulling us away from our true essence. This disconnect from our inner selves can leave us feeling less familiar with who we are, less confident, less loving and less able to trust or pursue what we truly want.

So how did we get here? And, more importantly, how do we find our way back?

This guide provides five essential steps to help you to reflect on your journey and rediscover your authentic self.

In these five transformative steps, based on my real-life experiences and concrete examples, I provide a clear path for young men to reconnect with themselves, achieve inner peace and encourage relationships built on respect, love and equality. This guide is a roadmap to creating a harmonious world where men and women thrive together, free from the confines of patriarchal and societal expectations. These steps brought me out of the depths of depression and have helped others to find their way back to themselves.

This is an invitation for you to embark on a transformative journey, empowering you to wake up and realise that the frames that have been holding you back are no longer there. This book will guide you towards self-discovery and freedom of thought, helping you to build a future where respect, peace and love are the core of your existence.

If you're ready to step into a new era, this book is for you. It speaks to those searching for a way out of the oppressive societal norms that align with the demands of today's world.

1. **Reconnection**: Begin by rediscovering your inner world – the place where your childhood dreams and desires once lived.
2. **Freedom**: Free yourself from the social constructs and expectations that have distanced you from your true nature.
3. **Peace**: Cultivate inner peace by embracing who you are without judgment or external pressure.
4. **Health**: Prioritise your physical, mental and emotional well-being as the foundation for reconnecting with yourself.
5. **Respect**: Honour and respect your unique self, and let this guide your actions and decisions.

By following these steps, you can start the journey of rediscovering who you truly are, restoring your sense of confidence, love and trust. This is the path back to living as the hero of your own story once again.

Chapter 1: Reconnection

How to Get Back on Track

As we grow up, we often lose sight of our true essence, gradually coming to believe that we're nothing more than the person others see – be it friends, family, peers or society at large.

While these perceptions can shape us, they can also confine us, causing us to forget who we truly are. Yet beneath the roles, labels and expectations lies a deeper reality, an inner truth that is uniquely ours. At our core, we're spiritual beings inhabiting physical bodies, and those physical forms mirror the thoughts and emotions we carry within.

Much of our outward behaviour, however, is moulded by external forces, namely social norms, cultural expectations and the constraining systems that surround us. These constructs, built up over time by collective beliefs and traditions, can offer structure but often impose rules that limit our growth. One of these frameworks is patriarchy, which prescribes how men and women should behave, feel and interact with the world. Although these traditions are woven into society, they are ultimately artifacts and old remnants of a world shaped by those who came before us.

Like any artifact, they are neither permanent nor above questioning. They can be revised, reimagined or even discarded completely and replaced by something new. Realising that you have the power to decide which beliefs and systems to keep, which to let go and which to construct yourself is the first step towards reconnecting with your authentic self.

In *Stolen Focus*, Hari explicitly warns us that modern life has pulled us further away from our inner selves. We stay hunched over our devices, yet we're disconnected from our own minds and hearts. Consider, for example, a teenager who once spent afternoons drawing or inventing stories only to swap those pursuits for endless scrolling in search of validation – with the intent of finding fulfillment or satisfaction in doing it. The result is an eroding attention span and a near-constant sense of external noise, which is difficult to get rid of.

How can we truly listen to our deepest desires and needs if our concentration is shattered every few minutes by a beep, buzz or notification? Reclaiming your focus and mental freedom is critical to rediscovering who you really are. It begins with reconnecting with yourself by dialling down that external clamour and turning inwards to ask, 'What do I genuinely want? What do I honestly believe? What am I truly feeling?'

Reconnection is, at its heart, a matter of choice. It's about your deliberate decision to look beyond the roles and social rules thrust upon you and to venture back to your innermost self.

If you reflect on your childhood, when you lived with minimal expectations and abundant curiosity, what activities brought you the most joy? Perhaps it was building sandcastles, inventing games or dreaming of becoming an astronaut. Maybe you loved filmmaking and creating movie storyboards, doing action scenes and shooting films with your mobile phone in real life with your classmates and friends. Those impulses were not mere childish games; they were clues to your unfiltered and true nature.

Now, imagine reshaping and transforming your life simply by realigning with that core essence, which holds your most treasured gifts, values and aspirations. Visualise a life where self-acceptance is not just an idea but a fully embodied practice. That means welcoming yourself without judgment or doubt and letting go of the weight of external expectations.

In her book *The Gifts of Imperfection*, Brown underscores this idea by writing, 'Authenticity is the daily practice of letting go of who we think we're supposed to be and embracing who we are.' This shift into self-acceptance can set you free, allowing you to nurture your abilities and trust your personal vision.

When you accept your flaws and recognise your innate worth, the truly extraordinary becomes possible.

By embracing your true essence, you tap into depths of creativity, resilience and potential you might not even have known you possessed. You can achieve far more than you might suspect, but it starts with giving yourself permission to act and do what you truly like. This small yet profound gesture of self-compassion can open doors to a life of infinite possibility. Ask yourself what life would be like if you lived unapologetically as your authentic self. What passions would you chase if you wholeheartedly believed in your own abilities? The moment you choose to align with your essence, you begin co-creating a life imbued with meaning, fulfillment and extraordinary promise.

When I was a child, my teacher put on a play. She gave me the main role and the chance to step up on the stage for my first time in my life. I learned by heart the role of a courageous girl who was independent, strong, free and a rebel. It was Astrid Lindgren's character Pippi Longstocking, who was rich and saved children from their parents and their rigid social environments. I felt that I *was* Pippi. The role was perfect for me, and I lived it authentically.

In my younger years, I felt like Pippi, standing up for the poor, the weak and the oppressed. But it was just a dream I could live in my thoughts because I, too, was growing up within rigid and patriarchal social norms. The story, however, remained in my heart. I still feel the freedom and the passion for breaking free of those limitations. I have long been shaped by my social environment.

Breaking past your limitations often requires courage to go your own way. And it requires a shift in your perspective. Imagine setting aside fear of failure, fear of rejection or fear of judgment. In true danger, fear can protect you, but in everyday life, it too often keeps you from the dreams and desires that define you. Only in a supportive environment do you have the choice to move beyond those fears and into a broader realm of possibilities. Look out for these environments and for the people surrounding you with love and support because freedom doesn't lie in conforming to expectations; it lies in questioning them, going beyond them and shaping your own life.

Begin by exploring your inner realm, where your childlike wonder, creative spark and wide-open imagination once flourished. That place, untouched by fear, still resides within you. Reconnection is all about rediscovering that unguarded space and letting it guide you towards a genuine sense of purpose. How do you do this? It isn't by checking items off a list, but through a gradual journey inwards. Go back to your childhood, find out what you loved to do and search for your inner purpose – all those things you'd love to do and engage with on your life journey.

Start with gratitude. Gratitude is the link between your current self and the self you long to uncover because it shifts your perspective from scarcity to abundance. There is always something to be grateful for. It could be a nice word, a smile from someone or just the fact that you can eat daily and have a dry place to sleep at night. Focusing on what you have right now – your breath, your health, your experiences – opens you to your internal world. This is why thankfulness matters: it quiets that nagging voice of *I'm not enough* and replaces it with *I already have enough, and I am enough*. Gratitude brings you fully into the here and now and into the present moment, where your authentic self quietly waits to be rediscovered.

Turning inwards is the next crucial step. Reconnection requires you to carve out moments to pause, breathe and listen. In the hush of those moments, you might hear the long-silenced echoes of your aspirations, creativity and real needs. These elements of your personality are not lost; they've simply been muffled by the relentless noise of daily life. Reconnection, then, isn't about looking outside for something new; it's about remembering who you've always been. Reconnecting each day helps you to stay focused. It prepares you for the day ahead, and it enables you to live in the present moment. When you consciously appreciate the present and direct your attention inwards, you'll begin to sense the stirrings of your most genuine self. This is how the journey takes root – by showing up for yourself with patience and letting the process unfold.

Let me level with you for a minute: if you're feeling lost, like no one really sees what you're going through, you're not alone. Bruce Perry and Maia Szalavitz talk about how rough environments or a lack of support can leave a young man feeling totally isolated, as if he has to handle everything on his own. In *The Rise of Superman*, Kotler points out how easily you can drift when you don't have a sense of direction or strong support. It leaves you with that hollow feeling. *What am I doing? Where do I really fit in?*

Then there's the pressure to act 'tough' or hold it all in, something Pleck calls 'the rigid expectations of masculinity'. Society is telling you, 'Don't cry, don't complain, just suck it up.' That can make you feel like you have to hide your real thoughts or emotions, forcing you to question who you are inside.

Yes, it's easy to look around and think that everyone else has it figured out. But they don't. A lot of us are just trying to find our way, even if we don't say it out loud. Sometimes, just knowing that you're not alone in feeling uncertain is a start.

Reconnection means reclaiming the self you've always been and choosing to live authentically. It involves lining up your life with your true nature rather than the person others believe that you should be.

Reconnection is not instantaneous, but each time you choose to listen closely to yourself, trust your instincts and honour the core of your being, you open doors you might never have imagined.

Your responses to the questions below will mark the beginning of this transformative path.

Are you prepared to take that first step? It starts, right now, with you.

> **How can you create space in your life to reconnect with your essence?**
>
> *If fear were off the table, what passion would you pursue wholeheartedly? And if you could shape your life and this world as you envision, what would it look like?*

Chapter 2: Freedom of Thought and Belief

Freedom of thought and belief is one of the most powerful rights we have as human beings. It's rooted in our core essence, a reflection of who we truly are. Across the globe, this right is enshrined in constitutions and laws, standing as a testament to the value of individuality and the universal recognition of our need to think and believe freely. But this freedom isn't just about external protections; it's about the internal permission we give ourselves to live authentically. We're given this freedom with the understanding that we use it to express our true selves. It allows us to operate as though everyone is respected for their beliefs and free to think as they choose – provided that we all act with respect and work towards the common good.

True freedom of thought invites us to explore and develop our own beliefs that align with respect, understanding and the acceptance of others. This doesn't mean abandoning our own truth; rather it's about embracing it while granting others the same space to do so. As children, we naturally believed in the impossible, trusted our dreams and lived with a sense of boundless potential. That belief was pure, untainted by fear or external expectations. You can reclaim your inner power by reconnecting with your essence – the part of you that knows who you are and what you stand for.

Think of your mind as a powerful force, like a mastermind. It responds directly to the thoughts you feed it. If you desire positive attention but act in ways that contradict that intention, this powerful force doesn't differentiate and simply follows the direction you've given it.

When you give space and time to a thought, your mind thinks that it's important and nourishes the thought. Each thought can lead to a clear outcome.

Imagine that you are driving along a narrow, twisty road. You are tired, you see a tree, you concentrate on the tree and your mind thinks about the tree, which is coming closer. You look at the tree and think that you'll hit the tree. And yes, you'll hit the tree.

In the words of Wayne Dyer, 'What you think, you will encounter.'

The mind listens to your actions, as it's paying attention to every movement you make. It enshrines your actions in your muscle memory and reacts accordingly. When you experience pain, it adapts your movements and tries to avoid negative consequences.

The mind is also a powerful storage centre for thoughts. It produces thoughts according to your memories and beliefs. The mind is capable of shifting realities for you according to the way that you think. For example, imaging lying in in bed at night and thinking negative thoughts about an experience from your workday. Let's say it's nagging, and the thought is not letting you go. But imagine telling your thought that this experience lies in the past and telling your mind to focus on an important assignment for the next day. You can imagine it successfully completed, and picture yourself being praised for it by others, thanking yourself for being so well prepared. You'll wake up in the morning with this last thought on your mind, looking forward to completing the assignment, and you'll see that the day goes by exactly as you imagined.

Vishen Lakhiani clearly shows that what you believe strongly will show up in your life. He explores this concept in *The Code of the Extraordinary Mind,* showing that behaviour is subject to unconventional laws that can redefine your life. If you think about something you really want, you can persuade your mind that it should follow that route. Thus, to truly harness this power, you must guide your mind towards self-affirming beliefs: *I am a person who loves doing sports. I am a person who is kind. I am who is capable of achieving big goals. I am a person who is worthy of abundance.* As Marisa Peer would say, 'When you think better thoughts, you change your life for the better.'

This freedom of thought is more than just a philosophical ideal; it's a practical tool for crafting the life you truly desire. Freedom of thought empowers you to choose your path with clarity, define your values authentically and determine the legacy you leave behind. Neuroscience shows that the brain has the ability to rewire itself in response to experiences and thought patterns. As Norman Doidge explains in *The Brain That Changes Itself*, our thoughts and behaviours literally shape our neural networks, which means that the way we think has a direct impact on the way we experience the world and create our future.

Free yourself from the social constructs and expectations that have pulled you away from your true nature. Liberate yourself from the constraints imposed by the outer world and turn inwards to discover who you truly are. Too often, we're shaped by the values and expectations of our social circles and families. We feel compelled to align ourselves with their beliefs rather than listening to the quiet truths that lie dormant within us. Be aware that only the truth within you, only your own thoughts and goals, will come true. Prepare yourself to live your life, living your dream and not the dreams of others. Impress only yourself and not those around you.

As children, we instinctively knew what felt right and wrong. We were confident in our choices and our approach to life. But as we grew up, adults taught us what to do and how to think, thus conforming us to societal rules and shaping us into specific moulds and role models. We were told that life is a struggle, that freedom is not part of it and that we must fight our way through. But why did we believe it and accept it as a truth? How did we come to believe that our lives must be confined to the limiting patterns that were told to us?

Now, as adults, we understand that the world is vast and diverse, with countless cultures and values. Different societies follow their own paths, and this knowledge gives us the power to step outside the boundaries we were taught. We can choose our own paths and reclaim our freedom to shape our thoughts and create our values and goals.

Think back on your own experiences. Have you ever agreed to do something – like drinking more than what you wanted – even though, deep down, you didn't want to? You might have gone along with the group only to come home feeling frustrated with yourself for ignoring your real desires. Moments like this shine a light on what freedom truly is: it isn't just about having options but about making choices that align with who you genuinely are. Terrence Real explains that men often feel pressured to appear 'tough', masking and suppressing their true emotions to meet society's expectations.

R. W. Connell and J. W. Messerschmidt delve into the idea of 'hegemonic masculinity', highlighting how patriarchal beliefs create a strict hierarchy of 'manly' behaviour that leaves little room for authentic self-expression. Way echoes this by showing how young men, under pressure to hide their vulnerability, end up missing out on the deep, supportive friendships they crave. Pleck describes this tension as 'gender role strain', a conflict that arises when boys and men realise that the rigid standards placed on them clash with their genuine feelings and desires. Ultimately, real freedom means honouring your own will and choosing a path that fits your true self instead of bending to external pressures.

However, such freedom is not automatic; it requires conscious awareness. This includes being mindful of your choices, questioning the beliefs you hold and understanding the influence you have on others. Lakhiani introduces the tool of 'visualisation', a practice that involves mentally rehearsing your desired outcomes with emotional intensity. According to Lakhiani, combining visualisation with a focus on gratitude and present-moment awareness activates the brain's reticular activating system (RAS), which filters information and aligns your subconscious mind with your conscious goals.

Neuroscience supports this. Studies have shown that visualisation can enhance motivation, improve performance and even lead to structural changes in the brain, as highlighted by Andrew Newberg in *How God Changes Your Brain.*

Visualisation can become a powerful instrument for your life journey. By vividly imagining the future you wish to create and aligning your emotions with that vision, you can prime your brain to recognise opportunities and take actions that lead to its realisation. The key is awareness of your choices, the beliefs you adopt and the ripple effect of your influence on others. When you approach life with this heightened sense of agency, you unlock a state of personal freedom that transcends mere existence. You become an active participant in your own evolution, crafting a life of authenticity and purpose.

Freedom of thought is not just about rejecting external constraints; it's about cultivating inner tools – like visualisation and self-awareness – that enable you to live a life of intention, clarity and impact. It's the foundation for your inner self-guidance.

We need to learn to trust our intuition. For that, we need to know 'the moments' of our authentic self. To find those moments, explore where and when you feel most authentically yourself. If you consider the moments when you most truly believe that you're 'you', note what you're doing and who you're with. These are the moments that reflect your truest self.

To get closer to yourself, imagine how life would be if every societal expectation fell away, and fear no longer had the power to hold you back. What dreams would you pursue? Who would you become if you were free to create your identity without constraints?

> ***Stop here for a moment.***
>
> *Really take a minute and think about it. What would your life be like if you followed your dreams and aspirations now?*

Neuroscience shows that such freedom isn't just wishful thinking; it's rooted in the brain's ability to reshape itself. Kotler, in *The Art of Impossible*, explains how the human brain, through the mechanism of neuroplasticity, can adapt and grow in response to intentional focus and effort, enabling us to break free from limiting beliefs and rewrite our mental mindset.

When you let go of external pressures and fears, you access what Kotler refers to as a 'flow state', a peak performance zone where you feel fully present, creative and capable of achieving your goals. In this state, your brain releases neurochemicals that enhance focus and increase motivation. These are the building blocks of transformation, allowing you to envision and create a life that aligns with your truest self. By vividly imagining the life you want to live, you train your brain to recognise opportunities and take aligned actions, as emphasised by Kotler and other neuroscience researchers.

So don't follow others blindly. Instead, choose to be the master of your own world. Be your own master and the creator of your life. Be aware of your footprints and the impact you leave behind. Neuroscience emphasises the importance of self-awareness as a critical component of self-mastery. As Daniel Goleman outlines in *Emotional Intelligence*, self-awareness involves recognising your emotions, beliefs and behaviours and understanding how they influence your decisions and interactions. This awareness helps you to take ownership of your life, enabling you to act with intention rather than reacting passively to circumstances.

But your journey is not solely about personal transformation; it's also about cultivating compassion and respect for others. Are you ready to reclaim that sense of limitless possibility and live authentically by your own beliefs? And – equally important – are you ready to honour and accept others for their beliefs, even when they differ from your own? Creating a better world starts with this dual commitment: striving for your own growth while working towards a collective vision of mutual respect and shared progress.

Living a life of intention, guided by your own values and aspirations, isn't just about self-empowerment; it's about contributing to a world where everyone can thrive. As Kotler reminds us in his exploration of human potential, our greatest achievements often come when we blend individual mastery with a purpose that serves others. Are you prepared to step into this possibility, to lead a life that is not only meaningful to you but also enriching to those around you? The choice is yours to make, and the tools to create that life are already within you.

If you could think freely about your deepest desires, with no interference from your social environment, what would you choose to have and who would you choose to be?

If you weren't held back by what others expected from you, what would you choose to do? Who would you choose to be if your deepest fears were taken away?

Chapter 3: Peace

Forgiveness as a Path to Unity

Forgiveness is not always easy, especially when the pain runs deep. But what if I told you that by forgiving, you are not only setting the other person free but setting yourself free too?

I want you to think for a moment about someone who has hurt you – perhaps a loved one, a friend or someone who should have cared for you. They might have said something, done something or ignored your feelings in a way that left you scarred. It's easy to hold on to that anger and let it fester. But the truth is that when we hold on to these wounds, we carry them with us day after day, letting them affect our peace, our joy and our relationships.

Imagine a time in your life when you felt let down by someone you trusted – maybe even someone who was supposed to protect you. Think about your father or another figure in your life who treated you in a way that didn't align with their words. They might have claimed to love you, but their actions told a different story. Perhaps they were distant, controlling or harsh. Perhaps they made decisions for you without ever asking about your needs, your feelings or your desires.

In their minds, they were simply being strong, perhaps thinking that they knew what was best for you. But the truth is that they didn't realise that you were your own person with your own path to walk, and that you had your own dreams and goals for your future. Very often, we blame ourselves for those situations, which means that we feel guilt, as we believe that we're the cause of the action.

Forgiving them doesn't mean excusing their actions; it means letting go. It means releasing the emotional burden that's been weighing you down so you can step forward into peace. When you forgive, you give yourself the gift of freedom. You stop letting their actions control your happiness or your thoughts. You stop carrying the heavy burden of anger and resentment, and you can release the blame and the guilt. You allow yourself to breathe again, to feel yourself again.

When we forgive, we make space for peace to flow into our lives. It's like taking a deep breath, feeling it fill you with calm and then letting it go – and letting everything else go with it. We don't need to hold on to the past anymore.

Forgiveness is the path to realising that we're all connected. We're part of something much greater than ourselves, a universe that existed long before we were born and will continue long after we're gone. We're part of a vast collective. Our individual actions, choices and feelings all have an impact on this greater whole.

When we release past hurts, we allow ourselves to connect with that greater whole. We realise that, despite our differences, we all share the same roots. We all come from the same source, the same universe, and each of us is a unique expression of that origin. We're spirits in bodies, here for a limited time, experiencing the world as humans.

Forgiveness is about letting go of the things that divide us. It's about recognising that the pain of the past no longer serves us. We have the power to choose peace instead of pain. The more we forgive, the more we become aligned with the flow of life and the more we contribute to the collective harmony of the universe.

So today, I invite you to take that step towards peace. Let go of the hurt, the anger and the resentment. Forgive not for them but for yourself. Free yourself from the weight of the past and embrace the unity that comes from understanding that we're all part of something much greater. We're all connected, and together, we make the world a better place.

As part of a greater whole, we must first release ourselves from blame and guilt, acknowledging that we, too, share in these burdens. This begins with forgiving ourselves. Self-forgiveness is not merely an emotional release but a transformative practice that enables us to break free from the weight of regret and self-judgment, clearing the path for growth and fulfillment. Only by liberating ourselves and others from the past do we open the door to forgiveness. Forgiveness, in turn, offers us the chance to begin again at any moment, inviting peace, tranquillity and love into our innermost beings.

Research in neuroscience supports the profound impact of forgiveness, showing that it reduces activity in the amygdala – the brain's fear and emotional response centre – and promotes activation of the prefrontal cortex, which governs rational thought and decision-making. In *The Body Keeps the Score*, Dr Bessel van der Kolk explains how unresolved emotions, like guilt and shame, can become stored in the body and influence our behaviour and mental well-being. By forgiving yourself, you can begin to heal and reframe your narrative, moving towards a life of purpose and wholeness.

As you reflect on these moments, you should also consider the influence of larger societal structures, like the patriarchy, which can subtly or overtly shape your worldview and experiences.

Often, patriarchal norms and the violence they perpetuate leave deep emotional imprints, fuelling negativity, blame and guilt. For example, if your father tells you what to do, how to behave and what your future is, you'll never experience what your true self intends for you. Should you resist, or should you not behave as expected, you'll be punished by distance and criticism instead of love. Should you give in to him, you'll live a life you never chose and experience things you never intended. With time, you'll forget who you are and what your own dreams were. Next, you'll change your thoughts, your beliefs and your behaviour. Finally, you'll start to believe that this version of you, the life your father wanted for you, is true.

Recognising that these oppressive systems can impact the way that you see yourself and others is crucial. By understanding how your personal story intersects with these broader forces, you open up space for genuine self-forgiveness and, in turn, a more expansive forgiveness towards others.

When you acknowledge the role that the patriarchy plays and the goal of violence – whether physical, emotional or structural – you begin to loosen the grip of blame. Rather than seeing yourself solely as a product of harmful systems, you begin to perceive these influences as part of the complex tapestry of your life experiences. In doing so, you grow more compassionate towards yourself and also cultivate a deeper sense of empathy for others who've been shaped by the same forces. This process breaks the cycle of negativity and creates an opportunity to rewrite your life narrative in a way that fosters healing, understanding and empowerment for everyone involved.

As you continue this reflection, take time to identify the most important lessons you've learned. Perhaps you discovered the strength to overcome adversity or recognised the value of authenticity, connection and compassion. Neuroscience underscores the fact that reflecting on these insights consolidates them into long-term memory, reinforcing their influence on your behaviour and mindset. As Dr Daniel Siegal describes in *Mindsight*, this introspection fortifies the neural pathways that support emotional regulation and self-awareness, empowering you to approach life with greater clarity and intention.

By listing your pivotal life events, both triumphant and difficult, you can start to see how even the most challenging experiences – including those shaped by patriarchal norms or violence – have contributed to your resilience and empathy. In alignment with Viktor Frankl's perspective in *Man's Search for Meaning*, finding purpose in these experiences – particularly the painful ones – fuels personal transformation and bolsters your capacity for resilience. This recognition not only reveals how you've been shaped by broader social forces but also underscores the power of forgiveness in liberating yourself from the grip of blame and negativity.

Crucially, forgiving yourself remains at the core of this process. It isn't just an emotional release but a transformative practice that breaks the cycle of self-judgment and opens the door to growth, fulfillment and peace. Reflecting on your past missteps or perceived failures in a spirit of compassion frees the mental and emotional energy needed to create a future aligned with your fullest potential. As you reframe your narrative, you equip yourself with the wisdom, self-compassion and courage to move forward unburdened by guilt, regret or the negative impact of constricting systems.

From this space of self-forgiveness emerges a state of being that Lakhiani refers to as being 'unf*ckwithable'. It's an emotionally clean mindset, one in which no past negativity, future worry or external criticism can disturb your inner calm. Whether shaped by patriarchal pressures or societal violence, those forces no longer hold sway over you once you realise that true peace is a choice grounded in how you perceive and respond to life's challenges.

Cultivating this inner peace begins with embracing who you truly are, free from self-imposed judgment or societal constraints. Imagine a serene, playful garden within you. If someone enters that space with anger or blame, you have the option to invite them in, share understanding and restore harmony or to let conflict disrupt the joy. This illustrates that peace is ultimately an *internal state*. You maintain it by handling every situation in alignment with your innate capacity for empathy, compassion and love.

By connecting the dots of your life journey, acknowledging the impact of larger social dynamics and practising forgiveness – both for yourself and others – you learn to navigate challenges with grace. In doing so, you rewrite your life narrative from one bound by negativity and blame in to one illuminated by understanding, empowerment and unwavering tranquillity.

Reflect on your own inner peace.

Do you ever feel weighed down by patriarchal norms or by people who've suppressed you, decided for you or blamed you? What does forgiveness really mean in these moments, and how can releasing blame help you to reclaim your inner peace on your own terms?

Chapter 4: Health and Identity

Your body is your temple, but it doesn't exist in isolation. In societies shaped by patriarchal norms, where certain appearances, behaviours or roles are prioritised over others, it can be challenging to maintain the balance that allows both your body and mind to thrive. True wellness doesn't just require healthy eating, regular physical activity and nourishing your mind; it also demands that you honour your authentic self, free from external pressures that might distort your sense of identity.

Embrace whatever activities make you feel alive – whether that's sport, music, journaling, reading, being in nature or being outside in the streets. These moments of genuine self-expression strengthen the roots of your identity. When you feel a profound alignment with who you truly are, you gain greater control over your thoughts, actions and habits. This synergy between mind, body and inner self is the cornerstone of feeling healthy and whole.

At the same time, recognise that patriarchal expectations, which are often internalised over generations, can subtly distance you from your true identity. When I was growing up, women traditionally stayed at home looking after the many children. The women who worked were considered poor – it was said that the man of the house didn't earn enough to provide for the family. As the man brought home the money, he distributed it according to his own needs. He decided how much to spend, where to live and what the wife and the children would do.

In my own youth, I looked up to my dad. He was able to live the life he chose, he came home when he pleased, he gave out punishments when he wasn't happy and he told us what to do and how to behave. As Alfred Adler showed, the importance of feelings of belonging lead towards behavioural adaptation and, in this case, submission to the male head of the household. Relationships within the family were aligned with traditional social norms.

When you're disconnected from who you really are, even the most diligent health and wellness practices can fail to bring lasting well-being. Reclaiming your sense of self amid societal expectations is crucial to reaping the full benefits of good nutrition, exercise and mental health support. By prioritising your physical, mental and emotional well-being, you pave the way for a deeper reconnection with your authentic self and a more balanced life.

Several authors underscore the ways that social constructs and pressures, including patriarchal standards, can shape your sense of identity and affect your well-being. Hari, in *Lost Connections,* highlights how feelings of isolation – which are often intensified by social media – erode our connections and contribute to mental health struggles. Recognising these external forces and cultivating healthy practices that reaffirm your individuality can help to counteract disconnection, fostering a healthier and more resilient sense of self.

For example, Hari discusses how people today, despite being more 'connected' than ever through digital platforms, are experiencing an increase in depression and anxiety. One of the reasons he points to is the decline of face-to-face human interaction and the superficial nature of online communication. Hari's argument is that humans need genuine, meaningful connections to thrive, and without these, we risk losing our sense of belonging, which is foundational for mental and emotional health. In terms of respect, when we lack these deep, real-world connections, it becomes harder to respect ourselves and others because we're no longer rooted in authentic, supportive relationships.

If we look into mental and emotional health, it's important to know that rigid social environments and suppression of our own feelings can harm our mental health. In *Deep Secrets*, Way provides insight into how societal expectations, enshrined in patriarchal norms, force young men to limit emotional vulnerability. According to these norms, men are tough, without emotions and rule as male dominators. This imposed structure doesn't allow young men to live their emotions or to be themselves. Not being yourself means that you restrict your ability to form deep, meaningful friendships, as you don't know who you are. This might contribute to the fact that you don't know how to connect. Way uses interviews with adolescent boys to show how societal pressures to appear tough and emotionally distant prevent them from forming close bonds with their peers. For instance, many of the boys Way interviewed expressed a desire to be open about their feelings but felt that they couldn't because of the pressure to conform to traditional masculine norms.

According to Way, young men also need to be able to show emotions in order to create healthy relationships. It seems that the pressure on young men to suppress their emotions creates a barrier to personal growth and authentic connections, both of which are crucial for building respect and self-awareness. This is directly tied to the idea that self-respect is rooted in emotional authenticity. When young men are unable to express vulnerability, their sense of self and their ability to respect others are hindered.

Similarly, we now have to consider the role of technology in shaping identity and societal norms. Suleyman argues that AI is not only reshaping the way we work but also redefining societal values.

As AI takes on tasks once performed by humans, people can lose access to meaningful work, thereby diminishing their sense of purpose and self-worth. This, in turn, can erode self-respect, since individuals who no longer feel relevant in society might struggle to see themselves as valuable contributors. Moreover, the growing automation of jobs risks deepening social inequalities, further undermining mutual respect across different communities.

Against this backdrop, patriarchal norms can magnify these challenges by prescribing fixed roles for men and women, thereby limiting the ways in which individuals can adapt to technological shifts. These norms can hinder authentic self-expression, making it even more difficult to navigate an AI-driven economy that increasingly rewards flexibility and creativity. As a result, those who feel constrained by societal expectations – whether regarding gender, work or identity – face heightened risks of disconnection and loss of self-esteem.

Sherry Turkle, in *Alone Together*, shows how digital tools designed to bring people closer can paradoxically create feelings of isolation. Many people, especially younger users, substitute face-to-face conversations with text messages and social media updates, which often results in superficial connections. Turkle's findings reveal that while digital interactions might seem convenient, they rarely satisfy deeper emotional needs. To foster genuine respect – both for yourself and others – Turkle emphasises the importance of in-person relationships that allow for trust, emotional vulnerability and authentic communication.

Similarly, Twenge's *iGen* highlights the fact that constant online engagement can undermine mental health and self-respect. Although the younger generation is indeed more tolerant than those before them, Twenge observes increasing rates of depression and anxiety linked to excessive digital device use. When young people are deprived of real-world experiences that build resilience and self-worth, they also find it harder to engage in respectful, empathetic relationships. This pattern underscores the importance of balancing technology use with meaningful offline interactions that nurture a strong sense of identity.

Beyond technology, broader societal pressures also influence how individuals perceive and respect themselves. In *I Don't Want to Talk About It*, Real illustrates the way that patriarchal expectations encourage men to suppress their emotions, often leading to silent depression. This cultural emphasis on 'toughness' not only damages men's mental health but also erodes their self-respect, as it prevents them from expressing vulnerability or seeking support. Real's work highlights the destructive cycle that results when authenticity is stifled by rigid gender norms – an issue that can become even more pronounced in a world where technology often rewards openness and collaboration.

Elliott's *Young Men Navigating Contemporary Masculinities* expands on these themes, examining how outdated ideals of masculinity contribute to disconnection and self-doubt among young men. Like Real, Elliott describes how many men feel compelled to present a 'tough' persona, masking their true selves and losing touch with their emotional needs. This disconnection not only undermines self-respect but also hinders the ability to form meaningful, respectful relationships. By highlighting the need for diverse and flexible expressions of masculinity, Elliott's research demonstrates that respect flourishes when authenticity is supported, particularly important in a technology-driven era that demands creative problem-solving and emotional intelligence.

Taken together, these authors underscore the ways that both technological advancements and inherited social norms – especially patriarchal expectations – impact our sense of self and our relationships with others.

As AI continues to evolve, pursue real, in-person connections. Meet up with friends and live a life within supportive communities that enable compassion and emotional openness. Meeting physically allows us to learn to respect one another. It is important to realise that others are different but still acceptable. In an ever-changing world, we learn that self-worth and mutual respect is becoming even more crucial.

Finally, when it comes to redesigning your life, establishing new habits is essential. James Clear's *Atomic Habits* provides practical advice on how to break unhealthy habits and create new ones. Clear suggests that bad habits can be eliminated by making them invisible or harder to access. For instance, if you find yourself spending excessive time on your phone, he advises leaving it in another room to reduce the temptation. This concept underscores the importance of creating an environment that supports your goals and values.

When I reflect on my own past, I realise how deeply my unhealthy lifestyle influenced my identity and my sense of self. In my twenties, I was trapped in a cycle of late-night outings, unhealthy eating habits and a dependency on social interactions that left me feeling empty, as all we shared was drinking together. Despite enjoying activities like skiing and spending time outdoors, I felt disconnected from who I truly was. This disconnection manifested physically and emotionally, and I found myself struggling with a lack of self-respect.

One day, I woke up and realised that something had to change. I knew that I needed to get back on track, but I wasn't sure how. I started reflecting on my youth, my childhood and the things I loved doing before this unhealthy lifestyle started. I realised that I had been following the wrong motivations, trying to fit into a group that ultimately didn't care about my well-being or my inner self. I had lost my self-identity while I was following the rules and values of others.

Living in fear of losing everything I had worked for only made things worse. I was stuck, and I knew that I needed to make a shift. So, I began to articulate what I wanted to become, what I needed to commit to and why it was essential for me. I wanted to live a life that honoured who I truly was, and that meant that I needed to start taking care of myself – mentally and physically.

I began to do the things I had loved as a child, like cycling, running in the woods, swimming, reading and eating healthily. I stopped smoking and got rid of my drinking habit. I was making small but powerful changes, and slowly, I started to connect with my body and mind again. It wasn't easy, but it was essential for my overall well-being. I needed to show respect and responsibility for my body because it directly reflected my inner health and identity.

It wasn't until I began to make changes, starting with small, positive habits, that I began to reconnect with my authentic self. This journey to self-awareness, emotional balance and respect for my own identity is ongoing, but it has been transformative in achieving a healthier, more fulfilled life. It has given me a clearer vision of who I truly am.

One of the things that really resonated with me were the teachings of Kotler, especially in his books on good habits. He says, 'Your physical health reflects your inner well-being, and by taking care of your body with respect and responsibility, you support your mental and emotional health. Remember: we are what we eat, and we are what we do. So, think carefully about who you want to be.'

This quote struck me deeply. I realised that everything I had been doing – like smoking, drinking and neglecting my body – wasn't just affecting my physical health but my mental and emotional state as well. If I wanted to be someone who was strong, confident and at peace with herself, I needed to commit to taking better care of my body and my mental health. In doing so, I could heal my body and my mind and rediscover my true self.

I began taking responsibility for my actions and making choices that aligned with the person I wanted to be. I stopped looking for validation from others and tried to get rid of unhealthy habits. I started seeking out the things that truly nourished me. Through this process, I learned that the path to peace and self-identity begins with self-care and making conscious decisions that reflect who we are at our core.

The journey to a healthier life and mindset begins with creating a clear vision for yourself and your health. Picture the person you want to become, the version of yourself that is healthy, confident and aligned with your deepest values. Visualise this future self, and then commit to behaving like that person today. You don't need to wait for the 'perfect moment' to start. The key is to act now, even in small ways that align with your vision.

Start by setting specific goals. Think about the healthy habits you need to form – whether it's exercising regularly, eating nutritious food or prioritising sleep. These goals should feel achievable and actionable. As Clear explains in *Atomic Habits*, achieving your goals isn't about grand, sweeping changes overnight but rather about small, consistent steps towards them. Every day, make tiny improvements that, over time, will lead you towards the transformation you desire.

One of the strategies Clear emphasises is the idea of a 'habit contract'. This is essentially a commitment you make with yourself to follow through on your goals. For example, decide what you'll eat for the week, how you'll work out or when you'll practise mindfulness. The key is accountability. Clear suggests integrating someone else into this contract – perhaps a friend or fitness trainer – who will hold you responsible for sticking to your commitments. They sign the contract with you, becoming your counterpart and ensuring that you stay on track (though, obviously, you can set up that contract or written goal just for yourself).

Let me share an example from my own journey. I was at a point where I knew that I needed to take control of my health, but I was struggling to make lasting changes. So, I decided to create a habit contract with myself. I signed up for a fitness program, committed to healthy eating habits and made sure to schedule regular check-ins with a personal trainer. This wasn't just about physical transformation but also about holding myself accountable for a vision I had for my life. And even when I didn't feel like it, having that commitment kept me on track – even on the toughest days.

Of course, change isn't always linear. As Clear mentions, we often fall back into old habits. Human nature makes it easy to slip back into comfort zones, to get distracted or to lose sight of the goal. This is why regular reflection is essential. We need to evaluate our habits and be honest with ourselves about our progress. Habits are powerful, but consistency is what makes them stick. Clear stresses that repeating a habit is key to building evidence of your desired identity. Every time you choose a healthy action, it reinforces the person you want to become.

This process is all about shifting your identity. Often, the beliefs we hold about ourselves are the very things that hold us back. If your identity is rooted in excuses, or if you see yourself as someone who 'can't change', then you'll constantly fight against progress. Clear points out that identity is at the core of what we do. If your identity is based on negative beliefs or past failures, you'll be stuck. As Clear writes, 'Your identity creates a kind of pride that encourages you to deny your weak spots and prevents you from truly growing.'

In fact, Paul Graham, cited in *Atomic Habits*, gives a valuable piece of advice: 'Keep your identity small.' When we define ourselves too rigidly – whether it's as someone who's going to become 'a great CEO', 'a perfect parent' or an Olympic gold medalist – it becomes harder to adapt and evolve as life and circumstances change. So, instead of tying your identity to a static title, shift it to something more fluid and growth oriented.

Instead of saying, *I am a successful CEO*, say, *I am the type of person who builds and creates things*. Instead of saying *I am a sporting champion*, say, *I love doing sports, as it clears my mind, helps me to get focused and keeps me healthy*. This opens up space for growth and learning, allowing you to adapt and move forward.

Ultimately, the journey to change isn't about perfection; it's about progress. It's about understanding that small, consistent actions lead to a new identity, a healthier you who is more connected to your inner self.

As you work towards this new self, remember that every step forward is a victory. By taking ownership of your habits and reflecting on your identity, you can shape a future that aligns with the person you're becoming. You can celebrate all your achievements and be grateful for what you've done and where your journey is leading you.

In this context, an interesting point of view comes from the legendary Chinese philosopher Lao Tzu, who teaches us that, in order to form our best habits, we need to create an identity that remains flexible and adaptable. Lao Tzu wisely told us, 'Men are born soft and supple, dead they are stiff and hard. Whoever is soft and supple is alive. The hard and stiff are broken, the soft and supple will prevail.'

Friedrich Nietzsche reminds us that, 'With a big why, you can overcome any how.' In other words, if your motivation and desire are strong enough, you'll find the strength to overcome any obstacle. The 'how' is the path you need to walk, but the 'why' is the driving force. If your purpose is clear – if your 'why' resonates deeply within you – then nothing will stop you from achieving it. So, choose your 'why' wisely. It needs to be something that fuels your passion and gives you the resilience to keep going even in the face of challenges.

Now, let's talk about how to find and fix your bad habits. Often, we have cravings or behaviours that we know aren't good for us, but we continue to indulge them. For example, you might crave a fatty burger with fries or a sugary cream cake, even though you know that it isn't healthy or nourishing. You understand that the burger won't help you feel better and neither will the dessert – and that you'll crave something else in an hour as neither one was nourishing.

If you pause and think about the 'why', then you discover the truth: the craving isn't about the burger or the cake itself; it's about something deeper. You're hungry, and you need to eat to survive. The craving is a symptom of a deeper need, not the need itself. This same principle applies to cravings for social behaviours like smoking or drinking. In these cases, we might feel the need to fit in, to feel socially accepted or approved of within a group of people who engage in these behaviours. But deep down, we know that we don't need to smoke or drink to connect with others. We don't need to eat sugary cake or fatty burger meals to be well nourished. We've simply learned to associate those behaviours with belonging and with certain emotions that we would like to have.

In today's digital age, many of us turn to social media in search of connection with others, to fill the void of loneliness or to seek external validation. But this often leaves us feeling disconnected and unfulfilled because there is a platform between humans and connection is artificial in some ways. *Can I trust in these messages, and do people really like what I post?*

The craving for connection isn't really about social media; it's about a deeper need for genuine relationships. This longing can often be masked by fleeting moments of external approval or by the kinds of connectedness we can find through belonging to a virtual group of people.

In a world buzzing with social pressure, non-stop uncertainty and the endless pursuit of things we don't truly need, it's easy to lose sight of who we really are. That's where inner peace comes in, which is an important built-in compass back to yourself. All it takes is a moment of stillness – a pause to observe your thoughts and emotions without judgment. As soon as you notice the chaos swirling around, simply turn inwards. In that hush, you'll find the clarity and calm that realign you with your most authentic self.

Meditation becomes a tool for grounding yourself – not as an escape but as a way to tune in to how present you are in your own life. It can help you to evaluate how connected you are to your true self – whether in your relationships, your creativity or your physical health. Meditation can actually improve things like sleep, mental clarity and even your sex life by reducing stress and boosting your dopamine and serotonin levels – the chemicals that trigger feelings of bliss.

Let's dive deeper into how these two chemicals work. Dopamine is often called the 'reward' neurotransmitter, associated with motivation and pleasure. It's the chemical that drives you to seek rewards and feel pleasure when you achieve something. Whether it's eating a satisfying meal or hitting a fitness goal, dopamine is what makes you feel good and motivates you to keep pushing forward. On the flip side, serotonin is known as the 'mood stabiliser'. It helps to regulate mood, reduces anxiety and contributes to feelings of calm and emotional balance. While dopamine is about the drive to achieve, serotonin is about contentment and inner peace.

Both neurotransmitters play a vital role in the way we experience the world around us. By maintaining a healthy balance between them, we can better regulate our emotions, stay motivated and find a sense of peace. But how do we steer these chemicals? The great news is that you have a lot of control over them.

You can boost dopamine by setting and achieving small goals. Every time you reach a milestone, your brain releases dopamine, giving you a sense of satisfaction and encouraging you to keep going. Whatever goal you have set up, if you reach it, you enjoy a certain satisfaction. The higher the goal, the more you get out of your comfort zone, the more sense of reward you'll feel. Importantly, it can be equally rewarding to engage in activities you like doing. That might be exercise like going to the gym, cycling or swimming or creative activities like drawing, playing music, painting, speaking or writing. All of these can naturally increase dopamine levels. On the other hand, serotonin can be enhanced by regular mindfulness practices like meditation, as well as by getting outside in the sunlight, eating a balanced diet and connecting with loved ones.

By making conscious choices to focus on positive behaviours that promote these chemicals, you can create a cycle of well-being that feeds your motivation and keeps your mood stable. Meditation in particular helps to regulate both dopamine and serotonin levels. It calms the mind, reduces stress and enhances your ability to remain grounded, which naturally supports your emotional health.

But it isn't just about feeling good temporarily; it's about becoming the kind of person who cultivates lasting peace and motivates themselves towards meaningful goals. As Clear points out, repeating a habit is essential for building evidence of your desired identity. Every small choice you make – whether it's a healthy meal or a thoughtful reflection during meditation – adds up to reinforce who you're becoming.

In the end, meditation, self-reflection and mindful action are powerful tools to help you to steer your dopamine and serotonin levels in a way that supports your growth. It isn't about seeking fleeting pleasure or external validation.

Instead, it's about creating a deeper sense of inner peace, self-connection and authentic happiness. By embracing these practices, you can transform your life and become the best version of yourself, aligned with your true identity. Life is far easier if you feel balanced, feel well in your body, and feel empowered and energetic enough to pursue your goals.

In summary, cultivating respect for yourself and your needs and understanding your cravings helps you to get to be yourself on a daily basis. It also helps you to understand how societal influences and digital environments – including social networks and gaming circles – shape our identities and relationships and how you can reshape them to align with your own goals, values and longings.

By developing an awareness of who you truly are, introducing new healthy habits, doing activities you like, prioritising emotional well-being and acknowledging the pressures that shape your behaviours, you can foster a balanced, healthy life rooted in self-respect and authentic connections with others.

Have you ever reflected on how your lifestyle and habits influence your physical and mental well-being?

Have you considered changing or introducing new habits to support a healthier, more balanced life? Do you believe that improving your health can play a key role in achieving your goals, living in alignment with your true purpose and building up healthy relationships?

Chapter 5: Respect for Yourself and Others

The Role of Social Constructs

Respect is a foundational element of any relationship, and it originates with self-respect: the act of acknowledging your individual journey, embracing your personal growth and honouring your values. Yet entrenched patriarchal and social constructs often erode this principle.

Patriarchy is a system where the male – often the father – is on top of the pyramid. He directs the family from the top down. The household or the members of the firm have to submit to the orders of the father or the patron.

Obviously, this sole decision maker induces inequality, limiting the rights of certain groups and forcing young men into prescriptive roles, as they have to submit to the father or the patron. But they also need to suppress women, keeping them in their limited roles. The consequences of this top-down system might not be understood while people are growing up. Young men might not realise what they are undergoing while being tough and disrespecting others because they have to obey the rules dictated by the patriarch.

By recognising that each person's life path is shaped by diverse experiences, we lay the groundwork for deeper understanding, acceptance and cooperation. This shared respect is important for creating communities that stand against entrenched injustices, ultimately fostering a more empathetic and supportive world.

Respect also encompasses the collective sharing of responsibilities and an acknowledgment of each individual's inherent freedom of thought and belief. It compels us to build nurturing and empowering spaces where people can uplift one another, actively confronting inequalities and systemic oppression.

In the quest for true equality, respect is pivotal in challenging the patriarchal norms that hinder us. It means that we can all lead fulfilled, valued and peaceful lives.

In professional settings, respect manifests as the empowerment of every team member. Such an environment relies on a spirit of collaboration, trust and genuine appreciation for the diverse contributions each person brings. By encouraging initiative and providing guidance as needed, we can cultivate a workplace culture in which everyone feels heard and respected. Team discussions should remain judgment free, with shared responsibility and a collective focus on achieving mutual objectives. This ensures that no one is held back, left out or excluded by oppressive social frameworks, and that everyone has the opportunity to bring their best selves.

Woodring's article 'The Effects of Social Conditioning on Behavioral Patterns in Early Childhood' sheds light on the early formation of behaviours and identities. From a young age, the way we're socialised shapes the way we interact with others, often leading to ingrained patterns that affect our ability to form healthy, respectful relationships. By understanding how early socialisation influences behaviour, we can better cultivate self-respect and apply it in our interactions, encouraging more empathetic and cooperative dynamics.

Hari, in his book *Lost Connections,* further explores how feelings of disconnection, shaped by societal expectations, lead to mental health struggles. Despite the digital connections available to us today, many people experience profound disconnection, which exacerbates feelings of purposelessness and isolation. When individuals feel disconnected from themselves and others, it becomes challenging to foster a sense of respect – both for their own journeys and for the unique paths of others. Hari's work highlights the importance of reconnecting, which is essential for promoting mental well-being and creating a more compassionate world where mutual respect thrives.

Social constructs play a significant role in shaping who we are. In *The*

Saturated Self, Gergen explores how modern life bombards us with competing influences. These influences – from media to societal expectations – can confuse and overwhelm your sense of self. As Gergen argues, individuals in contemporary society often struggle to define who they truly are in a world filled with multiple, often conflicting, expectations. This disconnection from a stable sense of self can hinder respect for your own journey and values, which in turn affects the ability to respect others. When we're unsure of who we are, respecting others becomes more difficult because we can be too focused on navigating our own identities in a saturated, judgmental world.

Jeffrey A. Kottler's *Beyond Blame* delves into the way that social conditioning affects our behaviour, particularly in the way we handle conflict. Kottler explains that individuals often internalise social pressures, leading to patterns of conflict where self-blame or misplaced responsibility take hold. These learned behaviours, shaped by societal expectations, prevent individuals from respecting their own worth and recognising their role in relationships. If we're conditioned to blame ourselves for conflicts or challenges, it becomes difficult to honour our own journeys and to engage in relationships from a place of mutual respect.

Nancy Folbre's *The Invisible Heart* takes this further, discussing the ways that economic systems and social norms shape the dynamics of family life. These systems, often taken for granted, influence how we relate to others and to ourselves. For example, traditional gender roles or economic pressures can create imbalances in power and respect within families and communities. Recognising these influences is a crucial step in developing respect not only for others but for ourselves as individuals worthy of dignity regardless of external expectations.

Ultimately, respect is rooted in our ability to honour ourselves and acknowledge the social constructs that influence our identities and relationships. When we understand how we have been shaped by societal influences, we can begin to break free from harmful patterns, foster a deeper sense of self-respect and create more meaningful, respectful connections with others.

Respect is the recognition of the inherent value in yourself and others. It's treating each person with dignity, fairness and consideration. It involves acknowledging differences, fostering open communication and encouraging both personal and collective growth.

Respect is not only about how we treat others but how we engage with ourselves. By honouring our true selves, we can respect the unique paths of others, leading to a more compassionate, connected and equitable world.

Have you ever thought about how respecting yourself impacts your ability to respect others?

In what ways can you foster mutual respect in your relationships and communities? How does sharing responsibility and allowing freedom of thought contribute to building a respectful, collaborative environment around you?

Conclusion

If you've made it to this point, it means that you're ready for a change.

Maybe you've spent years feeling trapped by the expectations of others – those of society, your family or your friends. Maybe you've questioned why life feels so disconnected from what you once dreamed it could be. This book was about giving you the tools to wake up, break free and reclaim your life.

Let's not sugarcoat it: the world can be tough on men.

Society tries to box you into roles and definitions that don't always fit. It tells you what it means to be a 'man', and most of the time, that means hiding your emotions, playing it safe and living according to someone else's script. The result? You lose touch with who you are and what you truly want. You start living a life that feels small, inauthentic and constrained.

But it doesn't have to stay that way.

You've always had the power to rewrite your story. It starts by recognising that the world's rules don't define you – you do. This book has guided you through five essential steps to reclaim your life: *Reconnection*, *Freedom*, *Peace*, *Health* and *Respect*. These aren't just ideas; they're tools to help you to take back control, make choices aligned with your values and build a life that feels true to you.

The first step is reconnecting with yourself.

Think back to when you were a kid, full of imagination and boundless potential. Back then, you believed that anything was possible, and you weren't afraid to dream big. That version of you still exists – it's just been buried under years of societal conditioning and the pressure to conform. Reconnection is about finding him again, listening to your inner voice and rediscovering the dreams and values that truly matter to you.

From there, it's about claiming your freedom to think for yourself, to act based on your values and to live without constantly seeking approval.

Society will always try to tell you how to behave, how to succeed and even how to feel. But you don't have to follow the script. You can choose your own way, and that choice starts now.

With freedom comes the peace of knowing that you're enough just as you are.

You don't have to fit into someone else's idea of what makes a 'real man'. You don't have to meet impossible standards or prove your worth to anyone. True peace comes when you stop measuring yourself against others and start appreciating who you already are.

Then there's health – and not just physical, but mental and emotional too.

How often do you prioritise your well-being? If you've been stuck in a cycle of stress, self-doubt or negativity, it's time to break free. Taking care of yourself isn't selfish; it's necessary. Your mind, body and heart need attention if you're going to live fully and authentically.

Finally, find respect for others and yourself.

Respect means valuing your dreams, your limitations, your boundaries and your journey. It means standing up for what you believe in, even when it's hard. It means treating yourself with the same kindness and consideration you'd offer to someone you care about.

Now, let's be honest and be aware of the fact that this path won't be easy. There will be setbacks, doubts and moments when it feels easier to fall back into old habits. But growth doesn't happen in comfort zones; it happens when you challenge the roles and expectations that have held you back and choose to move forward anyway.

The frame you've been living in isn't real. It's a construct – a set of invisible bars created by society, tradition and fear. It might feel safe, but it isn't freedom. True freedom comes when you decide to live life on your own terms, no matter what anyone else thinks.

As Carl Jung said, 'I am not what happened to me, I am what I choose to become.' You are not defined by your past, your mistakes or the expectations of others; you're defined by the choices you make today – the choice to step out of the frame and the choice to embrace your emotions, your individuality and your power.

This book is not just a guide but an invitation. It's an invitation to wake up, see the frame for what it is and step beyond it. It's an invitation to rediscover the life you've always wanted and the person you've always been.

You've been given the background, the steps to find yourself again and the tools, such as meditating and going within, reading, setting yourself goals and achieving them, playing or listening to music, reading, writing, painting and exercising in ways you enjoy – such as doing sports. Never forget the importance of creating strong relationships, too, and meeting up with people who make you feel like yourself and who want you see prosper.

Now it's up to you.

Will you stay in the frame, living a life defined by others? Or will you take the leap, embrace the unknown and create a life that's fully and unapologetically yours?

The world doesn't need another version of you that blends in. It needs the real you, the version that thinks differently, lives boldly and dares to be free. Wake up. Break the frame. Reclaim your freedom. Become the hero of your own story.

Your life is waiting. The question is, 'Are you ready to live it?'

Definition of Patriarchy, Social System

Patriarchy: hypothetical social system in which the father or a male elder has absolute authority over the family group; by extension, one or more men (as in a council) exert absolute authority over the community as a whole. Building on the theories of biological evolution developed by Charles Darwin, many 19th-century scholars sought to form a theory of unilinear cultural evolution. This hypothesis, now discredited, suggested that human social organisation 'evolved' through a series of stages: animalistic sexual promiscuity was followed by matriarchy, which was in turn followed by patriarchy.

The consensus among modern anthropologists and sociologists is that while power is often preferentially bestowed upon one sex or the other, patriarchy is not the cultural universal it was once thought to be. However, some scholars continue to use the term in the general sense for descriptive, analytical, and pedagogical purposes.

Source: Brittanica. https://www.britannica.com/topic/patriarchy, accessed 10 February 2025.

Bibliography

Brown, Brené, *The Gifts of Imperfection* (Hazelden, 2022).

Brown, Brené, *Daring Greatly: How the Courage to Be Vulnerable Transforms the Way We Live, Love, Parent and Lead* (Gotham Books, 2022).

Clear, James, *Atomic Habits: An Easy and Proven Way to Build Good Habits and Break Bad Ones* (Avery, 2018).

Connell, R. W., and Messerschmidt, J. W., 'Hegemonic Masculinity: Rethinking the Concept' in *Gender & Society* Volume 19, Issue 6 (2005).

De Beauvoir, Simone, *The Second Sex* (Vintage, 2010).

Doidge, Norman, *The Brain That Changes Itself: Stories of Personal Triumph from the Frontiers of Brain Science* (Penguin Life, 2007).

Elliott, Karla, *Young Men Navigating Contemporary Masculinities* (Palgrave Macmillan, 2020).

Eugster, David, 'The Great Liberalisation', (2018) https://blog.nationalmuseum.ch/en/2018/09/1968-the-great-liberalisation/

Folbre, Nancy, *The Invisible Heart: Economics and Family Values* (The New Press, 2001).

Frankl, Viktor, *Man's Search for Meaning* (Rider, 2011).

Gergen, Kenneth J., *The Saturated Self: Dilemmas of Identity in Contemporary Life* (Basic Books, 1991).

Goleman, Daniel, *Emotional Intelligence: Why it Can Matter More than IQ* (Bloomsbury, 2020).

Hari, Johann, *Lost Connections: Uncovering the Real Causes of Depression – And the Unexpected Solutions* (Bloomsbury, 2018).

Hari, Johann, *Stolen Focus: Why You Can't Pay Attention – And How to Think Deeply Again* (Crown, 2022).

Howes, Lewis, *The Mask of Masculinity: How Men Can Embrace Vulnerability, Create Strong Relationships, and Live Their Fullest Lives* (Rodale Books, 2017).

Kimmel, Michael, *Guyland: The Perilous World Where Boys Become Men* (Harper Perennial, 2009).

Kotler, Steven, *The Art of Impossible: A Peak Performance Primer* (Harper, 2023).

Kotler, Steven, *The Rise of Superman: Decoding the Science of Ultimate Human Performance* (New Harvest, 2014).

Kottler, Jeffrey A., *Beyond Blame: A New Way of Resolving Conflicts in Relationships* (Jossey-Bass, 1997).

Lakhiani, Vishen, *The Code of the Extraordinary Mind: 10 Unconventional Laws to Redefine Your Life and Succeed on Your Own Terms* (Rodale Books, 2016).

Millan, Dan, *The Way of the Peaceful Warrior* (HJ Kramer, 2006).

Newberg, Andrew and Waldman, Mark Robert, *How God Changes Your Brain: Breakthrough Findings from a Leading Neuroscientist* (Ballantine, 2010).

Nietzsche, Friedrich, *The Twilight of the Idols* (Penguin Classics, 2012).

Perry, Bruce D., and Szalavitz, Maia, *The Boy Who Was Raised as a Dog and Other Stories from a Child Psychiatrist's Notebook: What Traumatised Children Can Teach Us About Loss, Love, and Healing* (Basic Books, 2007).

Pleck, Joseph H., 'The Gender Role Strain Paradigm: An Update' in R. F. Levant and W. S. Pollack (eds.), *A New Psychology of Men* (Basic Books, 1995).

Real, Terrence, *I Don't Want to Talk About It: Overcoming the Secret Legacy of Male Depression* (Scribner, 1998).

Siegal, Daniel, *Mindsight: Transform Your Brain with the New Science of Kindness* (Oneworld, 2011).

Suleyman, Mustafa, *The Coming Wave: Technology, Power, and the Twenty-First Century's Greatest Dilemma* (Crown, 2023).

Turkle, Sherry, *Alone Together: Why We Expect More from Technology and Less from Each Other* (Basic Books, 2011).

Twenge, Jean M., *iGen: Why Today's Super-Connected Kids Are Growing Up Less Rebellious, More Tolerant, Less Happy – And Completely Unprepared for Adulthood* (Atria, 2017).

Van de Kolk, Bessel, *The Body Keeps the Score* (Penguin, 2015).

Way, Niobe, *Deep Secrets: Boys' Friendships and the Crisis of Connection* (Harvard University Press, 2013).

Woodring, Daniel Paul, 'Dethroning the Systemic Patriarchal Social System: A New Dawn for the Environment and Human Rights' (2020).

Coming Soon …

Unbound: Break Free, Live Your Life

How Patriarchal or Social Constraints Shape Us and How We Can Reclaim Our Authentic Lives

Excerpt from Unbound: Break Free, Live Your Life

In the mid-twentieth century, the patriarchy began to be challenged in Europe as women and men alike questioned traditional roles and their impact on personal freedom. Today, those same structures continue to undermine our ability to think freely, eroding not only individual potential but also the democratic values we hold dear. This book is a call to action for both women and men, a guide to recognising the invisible frames that hold us back and finding the courage to break free.

This isn't just theory. It's personal.

Looking back on my own life, from a childhood in Switzerland in the 1970s to the present day, I'm struck by how much has changed. The pace of transformation – be it social, technological or cultural – has been both thrilling and overwhelming. Growing up with black-and-white television as our only window to the world, it was unimaginable that one day we'd live in a world dominated by smartphones, social media, and 24/7 connectivity. Yet, despite all the progress, the social constructs of the patriarchy remain deeply entrenched, limiting our potential and disconnecting us from our true selves.

In my twenties, I fell into an unhealthy cycle of late nights, poor eating habits and a dependence on social validation that left me feeling empty and lost. Despite engaging in activities I enjoyed, like skiing and spending time outdoors, I felt disconnected from my inner self. I was living according to the expectations of others, trying to fit into groups that didn't value who I truly was.

That disconnection manifested in my physical and emotional well-being. I was stuck – afraid of losing everything I'd worked for but too trapped by fear and inertia to make a change. One day, I woke up and realised that I couldn't keep living that way. Something had to change.

I started reflecting on my youth and the activities that had brought me joy, on the dreams I once held, and on the person I had been before unhealthy habits and societal pressures took over. I realised that, in trying to follow the rules and values of others, I had lost myself.

The change wasn't dramatic; it was slow but steady. I began by reconnecting with the things I loved as a child: cycling, running in the woods, swimming, reading and spending time in nature. I quit smoking, reduced my drinking and started focusing on eating healthily. These small changes became the foundation for a larger transformation.

It wasn't just about physical health. By taking care of my body, I began to heal my mind and reconnect with my authentic self. Kotler's words deeply resonated with me: 'Your physical health reflects your inner well-being, and by taking care of your body with respect and responsibility, you support your mental and emotional health. Remember: we are what we eat, and we are what we do. So, think carefully about who you want to be.'

Those words became my mantra. I stopped seeking validation from others and started focusing on the person I wanted to become. I realised that taking responsibility for my actions, habits and choices was the only way to reclaim my life and live as I had always imagined, and to take what was given to me at my birth into my own hands.

The journey I've described isn't unique; it's universal. Patriarchal and socially constraining systems don't just harm women by denying them opportunities and autonomy; they harm men by forcing them into rigid roles that suppress emotion, authenticity and connection. For decades, we've been living within these invisible frames, often without realising how deeply they shape us.

This book is for both men and women. It's about understanding how patriarchal systems and rigid norms influence our lives and choices and how we can break free from those constraints. For women, it's a call to embrace leadership and authenticity without fear or apology. For men, it's an invitation to step outside traditional roles and reconnect with their emotions, individuality and true values.

Breaking free starts with small changes. It's about asking hard questions: *Who am I living for? Whose values am I following? What kind of life do I want to lead?* It's about making deliberate choices that align with our true selves and rejecting the expectations that don't serve us.

This book draws on my story and the stories of others, but it's also a guide for anyone ready to reclaim their life. Whether you're feeling stuck, disconnected or simply tired of living by someone else's rules, this is your chance to take the first step.

The world is changing rapidly, but the power to navigate that change lies within you. Let's break the frame together and create lives that reflect our deepest values and aspirations. This way, we can build a sustainable, respectful and peaceful environment where all humans can shape a trustworthy world together, and where opportunities are for everyone.

About the Author

Dr Jacqueline Kucera is social scientist and dedicated transformational leader striving to bring out the best in human beings. She evolved from the bottom to the top, from an overbearing patriarchal structure to a self-determined life and from a pharmaceutical sales-assistant to a PhD in social science. She possesses a strong combined skill set in sociology, leadership, human development, information management, data science and artificial intelligence. With her expertise, she seeks to promote human beings, teams and organisations, placing individuals at the centre and preparing them for a new era of work in a Volatile, Uncertain, Complex and Ambiguous (VUCA) world.

Also by Jacqueline Kucera

Wake up woman. It's your time to lead.

As we stand on the brink of a new era, where AI will be ubiquitous, organisations and their employees face unprecedented challenges in leadership.

These challenges present vast opportunities for transformation and growth, especially for female leaders. With these new, disruptive technologies, a new era is coming, where employees are free to work from home, further away from hierarchical structures, with increased flexibility in their working hours and access to a vast choice of information, tools and up-and-coming technologies.

More confidence and responsibility in the workforce will result in traditional hierarchies having a looser grip. However, flat hierarchies and consensus-oriented leadership do not prosper in patriarchal and top-down organisations.

Jacqueline Kucera demonstrates that together, we can shape a world that is not only advancing technologically but also deeply respectful, peaceful and empowering for all.

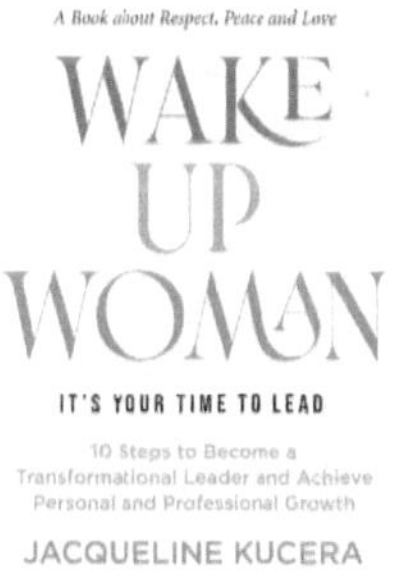

Wake Up Woman, It's Your Time to Lead

This book is an invitation to join a transformative journey empowering every woman to become her own leader. Through this book, you will embark on a journey towards self-discovery by forging a future where respect, peace and love form the core of your existence.

Top-down and patriarchal hierarchies no longer serve us. This book is for you if you desire to step into a new era. It speaks to those who are searching for more equitable and effective organisational models that align with the demands of the modern work environment.

Reading this book could change your life.

www.ingramcontent.com/pod-product-compliance
Lightning Source LLC
LaVergne TN
LVHW091344190726
843491LV00002B/876

9783952610220